OVERCOMING RECURRING PROBLEMS

Breaking the Chains that Keep Us Bound
to Recurring Problems by Spiritual Warfare

Melvin L. Johnson

Copyright © 2021 by Melvin L. Johnson

Overcoming Recurring Problems

Breaking the Chains that Keep us Bound to Recurring Problems by Spiritual Warfare

ISBN 978-1-7370418-0-1

All rights reserved. No part of this publication may be reproduced, distributed, or transmitted in any form or by any means, including photocopying, recording, or other electronic or mechanical methods, without the prior written permission of the publisher, except in the case of brief quotations embodied in critical reviews and certain other noncommercial uses permitted by copyright law.
Although the author and publisher have made every effort to ensure that the information in this book was correct at press time, the author and publisher do not assume and hereby disclaim any liability to any party for any loss, damage, or disruption caused by errors or omissions, whether such errors or omissions result from negligence, accident, or any other cause.

The names used in the stories and examples have been changed to protect the privacy of each person.
All scripture referenced has been taken from the King James Version.

Cover design: Ajao Ifeoluwa
Formatting: Ajao Ifeoluwa

First Edition 2021

Dedication

This book is dedicated to Ginny Tellez-Duran. She has worked diligently and long hours typing the manuscript. I thank the Lord Jesus Christ for her faithfulness.

CONTENTS

Introduction	6

SECTION I : THE PROBLEM — 9

Chapter 1 Recurring Problems Defined — 11

Chapter 2 The Make-Up of Man — 15

Chapter 3 Fear and Recurring Problems — 21
Fear of Panic Attack—A Recurring Problem — 23
Fear of Dogs and the Need for Specificity — 26
Fear of Grand Mal Seizure — 27

Chapter 4 Rejection and Recurring Problems — 31
Behavior of a Rejected Person — 32
How Parents Contribute to Rejection in Their Children — 33
Rejection Can Lead to Suicide — 35

Chapter 5 Control and Recurring Problem — 39
Timidity (Shyness)—And Recurring Problems — 41
Anger and Recurring Problems — 42

Chapter 6 Curses and Recurring Problems — 45
Occult and Witchcraft Curses — 45
Example of Occult and Witchcraft Curses — 48
Generational Curses and Recurring Problems — 50
Example of Generational Curses (Testimony) — 52

Section II : Solution Through Deliverance — 55

Chapter 7 Spiritual Warfare — 57

Chapter 8 Equipped with Spiritual Weapons — 63

Chapter 9 The Strongman and His House — 67
Identifying who the Strongman Is — 71
List of Strongmen in the Bible — 74

Chapter 10 Steps to Deliverance; Expelling of Strongman — 77
How to Bind a Demon or Strongman — 80
Application of Deliverance Principles — 82

Chapter 11 Recommended Action After Deliverance — 91
Pray for Healing of all wounds — 91
Renewing the Mind — 94
Bible References — 96

Testimonies and Endorsements — 99
About the Author — 105

Introduction

Have your recurring problems caused you to lose hope? Are you in despair and about to give up? The spiritual principles in this book will set you free and restore your hope. It shows how trauma from natural causes can be the doorway for spiritual problems. The traditional diagnosis and recurring problem are inclusive of mind and body. Seldom is spiritual entities ever considered.

We analyze both natural and spiritual causes of recurring problems. The spiritual causes cannot be seen or detected by X-rays, nor can they be seen with a microscope. These symptoms are manifested for everyone to see. The tree is known by the fruit it bears.

Many people find it hard to believe the roles of evil power in the life of mankind. Statements like, I don't know what came over me, I don't know what possessed me to do that, why that wasn't me, you know I don't act like that. These statements are reference to the existence of an entity other than themselves that is responsible for their behaviors.

As you read this book, you will learn techniques that will produce freedom in your mind, will, and emotions, as well as your body. These biblical techniques have proven successful many times throughout my years of ministry. Read the testimonies in the Testimony and Endorsement section. These true stories will ignite your desire to seek the freedom from any recurring problem. Purchase this book now and begin your journey to your freedom today.

OVERCOMING RECURRING PROBLEMS

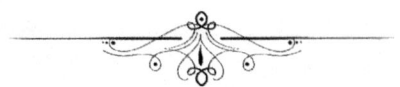

Section I
THE PROBLEM

Overcoming Recurring Problems

"
Understanding leads to freedom

10

Chapter 1

Recurring problems defined

Recurring problems are problems that happen over and over again at regular intervals. They may be caused naturally, or they may have a spiritual cause. Billions of dollars are spent on treatment each year.

Natural or physical problems can be caused by organism, bacteria, virus, fungus, or pathogen; Accidents, trauma caused by abuse, drugs, and alcohol use are examples ofphysical causes.

Spiritual problems can be caused by a demon's presence or demon infestation. The Bible refers to sickness caused by an unclean spirit, spirit of infirmity.

"And behold, there was a woman which had a spirit of infirmity eighteen years, and was bowed together, and could in no

way wise lift up herself." (Luke 13:11)

"And ought not this woman, being a daughter of Abraham, whom Satan hath bound, lo, these eighteen years, be loosed from this bond on the sabbath day?" (Luke 13:16)

"And he was casting out a devil, and it was dumb. And it came to pass, when the devil was gone out, the dumb spake; and the people wondered." (Luke 11:14)

Numerous statements uttered by man indicate his belief in an unseen entity affecting his behavior. Some of the statements are:

1. "I don't know what came over me."
2. "I don't know what possessed me."
3. "I don't know what made me do that."
4. "Why that was not me, you know I don't act like that."
5. "Did you see how he ran with the ball as if he was possessed?"
6. "He finally exorcised his demons."
7. "I just lost it."

A demonic presence exists between sickness, disease, and recurring problems. You can be free from recurring problems caused by demons.

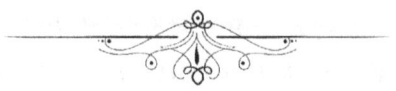

Overcoming Recurring Problems

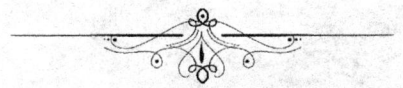

Overcoming Recurring Problems

"
*Spirit, Soul, and Body,
Not Mind and Body*

Chapter 2

The Make-up of Man

- Spirit, Soul, and Body

Man is made up of three parts, spirit, soul, and body. Three parts, one composite. The trichotomous model can be seen in the following scriptures.

"And God said, Let us make man in our image, after our own likeness: and let them have dominion over the fish of the sea, and over the fowl of the air, and over the cattle, and over all the earth, and over every creeping thing that creepeth upon the earth. So, God created man in his own image, in the image of God created he him; male and female created he them. And God blessed them, and God said unto them, Be fruitful, and multiply, and replenish the earth, and subdue it: and have dominion over the fish of the sea, and over the fowl of the air, and over every living thing that moveth upon the earth." (Genesis 1:26–28)

"For the word of God is quick, and powerful, and sharper than any two-edged sword, piercing even to the divid-

ing asunder of soul and spirit, and of the joints and marrow, and is a discerner of the thoughts and intents of the heart." (Hebrews 4:12)

"And the very God of peace sanctify you wholly; and I pray God your whole spirit and soul and body be preserved blameless unto the coming of our Lord Jesus Christ." (I Thessalonians 5:23)

A dichotomous model of man (mind and body) is often used in diagnosis and treatment. Where a dichotomous model is used, then one-third of the person is not being treated. Why treat man as if he were a three-legged stool with one leg missing? Recurring problems affect the whole man, spirit, soul, and body. The soul is the site of the mind, will, and emotions. We think with our mind, we feel with our emotions, and we choose with our will.

Problems in the soul and spirit of man can affect his body. Fear, stress, and anxiety take place in the soul and cause many problems in the body. The recurring problems that are labeled psychosomatic are problems caused by demonic activity. Such demonic activity cannot be treated with medicine.

The spirit is where we relate to God. It contains intuition, conscience, and communion.

The body is where we relate to our environment. It is the

site of the senses and the organs needed to sustain life. The spirit, soul, and body work in harmony with each other when we allow God to be in control.

The soul is the site of the will, mind, and emotions. The soul can be affected by recurring problems, unhealthy mind, damaged emotions, and a bound will. All affect the body, resulting in spiritual, psychological, and physiological problems and sickness of the whole man. These problems keep recurring until they are corrected.

The spirit of man lost fellowship with God when he obeyed Satan rather than God. He began to depend on knowledge from Satan and self-knowledge. Man declared himself independent from God, his creator. I can do it myself; I will obey whom I choose. Satan took advantage of Adam's disobedience. Adam by choice became a servant to Satan.

"Know ye not, that to whom ye yield yourselves servants to obey, his servants ye are to whom ye obey; whether of sin unto death, or of obedience into righteousness?" (Romans 6:16)

Mankind has continued a downward spiral since his disobedience and his servitude to "Lord Satan." As a servant to Satan, man's mind has been programmed with evil thoughts and behaviors. This programming is against the nature of God and dictates the evil behavior. This is the source of recurring problems. We need deliverance from the kingdom of darkness into the kingdom of light.

Recurring problems that take place in the soul of man can affect his mind and the total man. Emotions such as inferiority, insecurity, guilt, worry, doubt, and fears can cause frustration. One can become hostile, angry, depressed, and many other manifestations if these problems are not corrected. The hostility is a way of trying to express the pain and hurt that is felt by the victim. Often, the victim turns to illicit behavior in order to relieve the pain—the use of drugs, alcohol, sex, or anything that will relieve the pain.

Identifying the spiritual roots allows us to be effective with our treatment. Spirits cannot be treated with medication. However, they can be cast out. Deliverance has brought hope for many people.

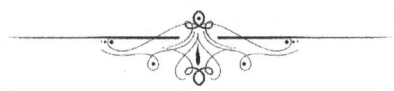

Overcoming Recurring Problems

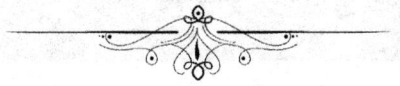

Chapter 3

Fear and Recurring Problems

Fear defined:

Fear is an emotion induced by perceived danger or threat, which causes physiological changes and ultimately behavioral changes such as fleeing, hiding, or freezing from perceived traumatic events.

Have you been diagnosed with a specific fear or anxiety disorder? Was the diagnosis for body and mind? Was the spirit included? The root cause can be trauma that created a doorway for unclean spirits to enter. What does the Bible have to say about fear? Fear is the opposite of faith. Little faith results in much fear. Peter walked on water until FEAR came upon him. When fear came in and replaced faith, he began to sink. Peter cried out saying, "Lord save me."

"And immediately Jesus stretched forth his hand, and caught him, and said unto him, O thou of little faith, wherefore didst thou doubt?" (Matthew 14:31)

Overcoming Recurring Problems

The Lord Jesus is able to save you from all of your fears. Fear can cause that which you greatly feared to come upon you.

"I sought the Lord, and he heard me, and delivered me from all of my fears." (Psalms 34:4)

"For the thing which I greatly feared is come upon me, and that which I was afraid of is come unto me." (Job 3:25)

"For God hath not given us the spirit of fear; but of power, and of love, and of a sound mind." (ll Timothy 1:7)

"There is no fear in love; but perfect love casteth out fear: because fear hath torment. He that feareth is not made perfect in love." (I John 4:18)

God has not given us a spirit of fear. Fear is given to us by Satan. The iniquities (sin) of the Forefathers are passed down from generation to generation. Generational sin is passed down through the bloodline. Inherited iniquities through the bloodline can be a source of fear and recurring problems. These recurring problems can be dealt with by deliverance. The only fear we are to have, is reverence of God. Reverence of God causes us to obey him.

"Thou shalt not bow down thyself to them, nor serve them: (other gods) for I the Lord thy God am a jealous God, visiting the iniquity of the fathers upon the children unto the

third and fourth generation of them that hate me." (Exodus 20:5)

Fear of Panic Attack— A Recurring Problem

I met Bob and his wife Betty in 1984. He was an Advertising and Marketing Executive. She was a former Rodeo Queen, now working as a freelance writer. They authored an article about Liberty Group Home, a Christian home founded by me. The Group Home provided shelter, food, and counseling for those who were suffering from rejection, homelessness, and other problems related to drug and alcohol abuse and rejection.

Bob and Betty learned about the Group Home and did a beautiful job writing about it. At the close of the Group Home, I opened Brother Mel's Southern Style BBQ restaurant, which we owned and operated for nearly 30 years. Bob did a marketing survey for Brother Mel's BBQ sauce, which helped us launch our sauce for distribution in the local stores.

A number of years passed, and I had not seen Bob. One day Bob showed up at the church that I was pastoring, All Nations Church and Deliverance Center, Fort Collins, Colorado. I was excited to see him and invited him into my office. We struck up a conversation, then he told me of a problem that he had.

He had sought help through the secular community as well as The Faith Community. No one had been able to help him. He stated that he had been listening to my radio program teaching about overcoming recurring problems by spiritual warfare. Bob considered his problem might have spiritual roots and said, "That is why I came to see you."

"What is your problem?" I asked. He responded, "I am a pilot, and I own my plane. I have been flying for a number of years. My problem is I suffer from major panic attacks while flying. The attacks have become so severe that I don't fly anymore. I grounded myself for fear of crashing."

I asked, "Bob, what happened just before the onset of the panic attacks?" He answered, "Whenever I would see an approaching cloud, a rain cloud, a storm cloud, or just a normal cloud, I would get scared. As I got closer to the clouds, fear would grip me. I would shake and break out in a sweat. My palms would become wet, my breathing would increase, and my heart rate would begin racing.

When the panic attack set in, I would quote scripture, 'God has not given me a spirit of fear, God has not given me a spirit of fear, God has not given me a spirit of fear.' All the time I was shaking and so, so, so afraid. I feared loss of control and crashing; yet I continued quoting scripture, 'This too will pass, this too will pass, this too will pass.' I did all that I had been taught to do, yet I was experiencing a panic attack. My plane is currently grounded, and it is sitting in the hanger."

I prayed, "Lord, please show me how to help my friend." I wasn't going to give him another scripture to quote. I asked Bob to come back in a week. I also told him to make a list of things that could be root causes of his fear and panic attacks.

Bob arrived early for his next appointment. He was excited about what the Lord had shown him about the root causes for his panic attacks. What do you the reader think the root causes were?

Bob and Betty had only one child, a son. Bob and Betty loved Billy. Bob would do anything for Billy. The day of the storm, Billy was left at home mowing the lawn on a riding mower. Bob left for the nearby golf course to play a round of golf.

A violent storm passed through the town. It passed directly over the golf course where Bob was playing. A sudden feeling of danger for his son came upon him. Bob rushed home to find his son frozen with fear, sitting on the riding mower. Bob grabbed his son in his arms, turned off the mower, and ran into the garage where they were both safe from the storm.

The trauma from the above events opened doorways for an unclean spirit of fear to enter into Bob's soul. The emotions and their manifestations are now subject to a spirit of fear. When the spirit of fear was triggered, all symptoms of fear began to operate, and panic set in. When the unclean spirit invades the soul of man, the spirit of fear acts as a catalyst to produce it's evil results, psycho-logical, physiological, and spiritual. The root cause of Bob's fear was dying and leaving his son orphaned, without a dad. Bob's fear was rooted in the fear of death, which would leave his son fatherless.

More about how to deliver Bob from the spirit of fear of death in Section II.

Fear of Dogs and the Need for Specificity

Praying against fear can be frustrating when you have prayed multiple times without getting any results.

A mother of two children, and a member of the local church, was in the office for prayer almost weekly. She wanted prayer for fear. She wanted freedom from the torment in her mind.

This particular Sunday afternoon, we entered into the prayer room determined to have success. The anointing of the Holy Spirit was upon me, and as we prayed, the unclean spirit began to manifest. The lady being prayed for fell to the floor and assumed a fetal position. As I continued to pray, I heard a sound coming from her mouth, yep, yep, yep. It was the sound of a dog, of course there was not a dog present.

As I prayed, the Lord Jesus Christ revealed to me that we were dealing with a spirit of fear of dogs. When we addressed the spirit of fear of dogs, she was set free.

What was the cause of fear of dogs? At five years old, the child came home from school to her babysitter's house. She had just started going down the stairs into the basement when the pet dog ran up to her. The pet dog jumped up and put his paws upon her shoulders. This frightened her very much. She yelled out and began to cry until she was rescued, thus creating a fear of dogs.

The trauma from the incident opened a doorway for a spirit of fear of dogs to enter her. This fear of dogs was reinforced by her seeing a dog killing a chicken by shaking the chicken to death. The fear of dogs remained in her until the spirit of fear of dogs was cast out, many years later.

In this situation, it was not adequate to just pray against fear. We were successful only after we identified the specific fear; we identified the fear of dogs, then we cast it out by name.

Fear of Grand Mal Seizure

Susan was an active and faithful church member with two boys about the age of my son. She became a member of the Church through Campus Bible Study at CSU.

Susan's recurring problem was epilepsy and grand mal seizures. She lost her job and license to drive because of the epilepsy and grand mal seizures. A grand mal seizure is the most dramatic type of an epileptic seizure and can cause an abrupt loss of consciousness.

Susan was asked to come up to get prayer. The Holy Spirit had told me to call her and tell her that tonight was the time for her healing. We prayed against grand mal seizures and for her to be healed. She left church and went home feeling better. She called me days later. All the symptoms of a grand mal seizure were upon her. I prayed against fear of seizure and the seizure stopped and everything reversed itself. Susan later told me that was the only time she had gone that far into a grand mal seizure and immediately came out of it, without losing conscience. We learned that the fear of having a grand mal seizure triggered the onset of a seizure.

Within 12 months, she qualified for her driver's license, bought a car, and was back to work after a long dry spell.

Job said,

"For the thing which I greatly feared is come upon me, and that which I was afraid of is come unto me." (Job 3:25)

Fear triggered a response in the one who was afraid. The spirit of fear must be cast out for freedom

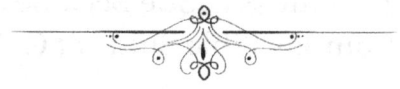

Overcoming Recurring Problems

"

The Inability to Show

Meaningful Love

CHAPTER 4

REJECTION AND RECURRING PROBLEMS

Feeling rejected is one of the most hurtful of human emotions. Rejection says, "You are not wanted, you are not acceptable, useless, or a castaway." Rejection is like an octopus with giant tentacles, able to affect you in many different ways.

Rejection has its roots in not receiving meaningful love as a child during the informative years. The lack of meaningful love opens the doorway for a spirit of rejection to enter. The spirit of rejection allows other unclean spirits to enter also. These spirits work together.

If you have not received love, then you don't know how to give or share love. The inability to show love allows an unclean spirit to enter. The unloving spirit causes more rejection. He tells you that you are unworthy or that you are incapable of being loved.

The unloving spirit works with the spirit of rejection to make the rejected person suspicious of any attempt to show him love. There is absolutely no trust in anyone. You don't really love me, what do you want from me, nobody likes me—the unloving spirit tells (the voices in his mind) the unloved person what he is already feeling. A wall is built up to protect him from more hurt. The wall acts as a thermos. It keeps hurt in and love out.

This strongman of rejection causes the rejected person to reject the very person that loves him. "I will reject you before you can reject me." Eventually you push the very person that loves you out of your life, isolating you even more, causing more rejection.

Behavior of a Rejected Person

The spirit of rejection tells him:
- You are unwanted.
- You are unlovable.
- You are unworthy.
- You are a castoff.
- You are stupid.
- You can never do anything right.
- The differences with others because of misunderstanding will never be reconciled.
- Fear of rejection.
- Fear of men.

- Fear of failure.
- You are not able to receive and give love.
- You need to be part of the group, hoping to find acceptance.
- Self-introspection—You are looking inside to see what is wrong with you (approval and acceptance from others).

The rejected person in the church wants:

A. Identity

B. Title

C. Status

D. Recognition

- Need for man's approval rather than God
- Trust—cannot trust anyone
- No self-worth
- Loss of identity

How Parents Contribute to Rejection in Their Children

The lack of proper nurturing can cause rejection in a child. Common statements heard by the child are:

- You will never amount to anything.

- Can't you do anything right?

- You are a dumb, dumb.

- I can never do enough to please mom or dad, no matter how I try; So what's the use trying?

The power of the spoken word penetrates the child's mind and the soul. Childhood rejection causes damage in a child's soul that follows him into his adult life. When parents bring their children for counseling, I ask the parents, "What have you done to this child that he needs to be seeing me?" The parent response often is, "I brought him to see you for help. He needs the help not me, just get him well."

Every person needs to be loved and accepted. When a child is rejected because of who he is, he will perform for acceptance. The problem with performance-based acceptance is you are never able to perform good enough to be accepted. The scale of expectation keeps changing. You do five units worth of work, then the scale is moved to ten units more, then fifteen units more, etc.—never good enough for a controlling parent who may be dysfunctional himself. The child feels, "I am damned if I do and damned if I don't."

Soon the child becomes angry, resentful, and unforgiving, and a root of bitterness develops in him. The pain of rejection becomes so great the rejected child seeks relief. He or she might turn to drugs, alcohol, sex, gang membership, and the occult as he seeks relief from the pain.

Rejection Can Lead to Suicide

The rate of death by suicide is on the rise, especially among youths. The spirit of suicide has many components. The strongman is usually a spirit of rejection. The spirit of rejection acts as a gatekeeper allowing other spirits to come in. When rejection happens at an early age, the young child tries to make sense of what has happened. His cognitive skills have not been fully developed, and he does not know how to handle the abuse. The abuse may be verbal, sexual, or physical. The abuse and rejection could originate from parents, siblings, teachers, pastors, or even other persons of authority.

Word curses hurled at the child, over and over again, begin to be accepted as truth, and the child begins to act out the behavior. "I wish you had never been born." The child hears, "I was a mistake." "I hate you; you are just like your dad." This becomes, "I am bad like my dad."

"You are a dumb-dumb," becomes "I am dumb and will never learn." "You are no good," becomes "No one loves me, I am unwanted." "You can never do anything right," becomes "It is never right no matter how I try. No matter what I do I can never please my father or mother." Unclean spirits are assigned to reinforce the hurts and trauma of the abused. They also maintain the wounds. They are lying spirits or accusing spir-its that often take on the same name as the hurt.

An unworthy feeling is reinforced by a "spirit of uncleanliliness"; now you have the damaged emotions plus an unclean spirit operating in you. This pattern repeats itself over and over again with every damaged emotion.

The pain of the rejection can last for years. In an attempt to relieve the pain and fill the void, the person (who is no longer a child), turns to alcohol, drugs, sex, gang membership, etc. Eventually a spirit of death by suicide enters. This spirit may lay dormant for a while. The spirit of suicide convinces the hurting person that the only way to escape the pain is to take his own life; "After all, no one loves me or wants me, I would be better off dead." Finally, the person takes his life.

An example of this is Joe, who was highly motivated to please his father.

Joe was highly motivated to please his father. He would do almost anything to gain acceptance from his father. The rejection Joe felt from his father was overwhelming. Joe didn't want to work in the construction industry, but Joe's father begged him to follow in his footsteps. Joe spent years going to college, he was a professional student. He received an associate degree from a two-year community school. He continued his education and earned a BS degree from a four-year college. Joe also had an MS and a PhD degree. When I met Joe, he was working on a post PhD fellowship program. Joe worked many years as a high school counselor.

The last report received was Joe had committed suicide. Joe's recurring problems resulted in him taking his life. We have delivered many souls from a spirit of death by suicide. The root cause was rejection from a controlling father. Learn how to overcome recurring problems from controlling spirits. You don't have to take your life because of the controlling spirits, because they can be cast out.

Joe sought help, but the spiritual component was not addressed. No one goes out and takes their life without giving it any thought. This is an example of rejection by parent, friends, or society.

Overcoming Recurring Problems

Control the Ultimate Form of Selfishness

Chapter 5

Control and Recurring Problems

*In the 1966 movie, Born Free, an orphaned lion cub was taken into the home of George and Joy Adamson. They raised the cub as a friend and a pet. They enjoyed the cub, named Elsa. Elsa became a domestic pet, and everything that Elsa needed was provided, including food.

When the Adamson's had to leave Africa, they had to leave Elsa behind. However, there was a problem with leaving Elsa behind. She had become a "non-lion." Elsa had never killed to eat. Without this skill, she would surely die from starvation. Elsa did not know how to sustain herself, as everything had always been provided for her. Elsa had to be trained to behave like a lion in order to survive.

Parents are you aware of how much you contributed to the dysfunction of your child?

*Joy and George Adamson, movie **Born Free** 1966

Parents, have you made your child a "non-person" by your authoritative and controlling way of rearing your child? Are you doing everything for your child out of control? Do you allow him to make decisions for himself? Is he encouraged to work and play independent of you? When all of the kids in your neighborhood are riding bikes, do you tell him he cannot have one yet? The message you're sending your child is that he is not capable of riding a bike like the other neighborhood children. Is he to be seen and not heard?

Does he have behavioral, emotional, or social problems brought on by your micro-management? Has it ever occurred to you, as a parent, that you may be a part of the problem due to the "strongman and spirit of control" that needs to be cast out of you? You might say, "Why it runs in the family. My dad was controlling, my grandpa was controlling, and his dad was controlling. It runs in the family." This describes a generational curse that can be broken. De-junk yourself, and you will be able to see clearly how to provide the help your family's needs.

It is the desire of the author of this book to make you aware and provide tools whereby you can be an overcomer and no longer be a victim. We offer a unique and powerful biblical solution. See Section II in this book.

Timidity (Shyness)—And Recurring Problems

Timid means shy and nervous; without much confidence, easily frightened.

Perhaps you have known a person who was quiet and shy all their life, one who had difficulty speaking up in public, classrooms, playground, church gathering, etc. She was always being bullied. She was the last to be invited to join any activity. In her heart, she wanted to be invited more than anything. The rejection was so great, she carried the hurt and found no resolution. When taken to the doctor for a physical examination, no known physical problem was found. She passed all of the tests.

Sue was raised in a controlling environment where she was to be seen and not heard. She was often sent to her room when she disobeyed. Soon Sue learned to keep her mouth closed to escape punishment. Sue grew up without a voice in anything that was important to her. She was bound in isolation. When Sue felt safe and was one-on-one with you, she would talk your head off. She never stopped talking.

The trauma caused by the controlling parent allowed a

spirit of timidity to come into her soul. Over a period of time, a dumb spirit entered taking her voice. These two spirits worked in tandem to produce a shy person who seldom spoke. After a confrontation, she wondered why she had not spoken up in her defense.

What was the cause of Sue's recurring problem?

1. _____

_____

2. _____

_____

3. _____

_____

Satan takes advantage of all kinds of abuse, spiritual abuse, psychological abuse, and physiological abuse, to keep the person from the destiny that God has for him.

Anger and Recurring Problems

Anger is an emotion that is allowed, providing the anger does not cause wrath or rage. Wrath is the action resulting from our anger. Wrath is kicking a door, putting a hole in the drywall with your fist, physical abuse to wife or children, or harm to yourself. Do not allow anger to cause you to sin. Sin is not acceptable to God. Disobedience to God opens a doorway for a spirit of anger to come in. Anger needs to be resolved before the sun goes down. Repeated anger without resolution of the problem can become a doorway for a spirit of anger to enter you, then anger is no longer just an emotion. It becomes an emotion controlled by a spirit of anger (demon). Often the person will say, "That behavior wasn't me," or "Something came over me and I just lost it." Indeed, you were being controlled by a spirit of anger.

"Be ye angry, and sin not: let not the sun go down upon your wrath." (Ephesians 4:26)

Anger is an expression of the emotions toward the controlling person. These emotions have been stuffed because a show of anger was not allowed. When the right trigger is pushed, all the suppressed emotion of anger surfaces and you have recurring problems.

The controlling parents are loved because of what they have done to help the child but hated because of what has been done to the child. The child is unable to forgive because of the pain. He may use the anger to protect himself from further hurt. Get ready to enter into freedom from this recurring problem.

"*Beware of the Company You Keep, or You May Be Facing a Wolf in Sheep's Clothing*

Chapter 6

Curses and Recurring Problems

Occult and Witchcraft Curses

Anyone that hates you enough to use witchcraft and the occult to curse you is definitely in a dark place. This person, whether he knows it or not, is working as a medium of Satan to perform Satan's evil and diabolic works. The people using witchcraft and occult as means to curse are servants of Satan.

"For such are false apostles, deceitful workers, transforming themselves into the apostle of Christ. And no marvel; for Satan himself is transformed into an angel of light."
(II Corinthians 11:13–14)

Satan desires is to snare your soul for use in his kingdom of darkness. He is an equal opportunity employer.

"Be sober, be vigilant; because your adversary the devil, as a roaring lion, walketh about, seeking whom he may devour." (I Peter 5:8)

May he devour you?

The word curse as a noun means a solemn utterance intended to invoke a supernatural power to inflict harm or punishment on someone or something. The verb, cursed, is to wish or invoke evil or calamity, injury, or destruction upon the victim.

Words uttered with the purpose of causing evil, calamity, injury, or destruction upon anybody is a curse. This kind of curse is spoken by someone else. Self-imposed curses could be uttered by a person toward himself. An elaborate ritual is not always needed to curse a person. A curse can be as simple as wishing ill will on someone.

Job said, "that which I feared most, has come upon me." A curse can be words that become a self-fulfilling prophecy. I must be accident prone, I will never make it, or I am not good enough.

"But the tongue can no man tame; it is an unruly evil, full of deadly poison. Therewith bless we God, even the Father; and therewith curse we men, which are made after the similitude of God. Out of the same mouth proceedeth blessing and cursing. My brethren, these things ought not so to be." (James 3:8–10)

It is important that we learn how to guard what comes out of our mouth. We may be speaking a self-imposed curse, or we may be cursing a loved one, a family member, or friend.

If you have been snared in the devil's web and you want freedom, the principles taught in this book will make freedom possible. I recommend you seek help from an experienced person of faith that understands his authority in deliverance to help you with this journey out of occult and witchcraft bondage.

The devil's servants have taken part in ceremonies containing rituals that give them power to curse. It is necessary that all known rituals be renounced. Not only is power gained by performing these rituals but also protection for them.

When one has been exposed to curses from an occult or witchcraft practitioner, it is needful to renounce any ceremony that has been used to gain power over them.

We have found it helpful to include in the renouncing prayer:
- I renounce all ceremonies and demonic rituals used by the person that cursed me. (Be as specific as you can.)
- I renounce all blood sacrifices both human and animal offered to Satan to gain power over me.
- I renounce the burning of candles.
- I renounce rituals dances.
- I renounce the pentagram and other Satanic symbols.

- I renounce drinking potions of any kind.
- I renounce oaths taken.
- I renounce sex orgies.
- I renounce use of drugs to create an alternate state of consciousness.

You may or may not have been an active participant yourself. The renouncing destroys the power of the enemy and aids in setting you free. Now follow the directions given in Section II, Solutions Through Deliverance.

God has given all men a free will, but all men's will is not free. Some men's will is held captive by the devil. You may have the want to do and still not choose to do. If your will is bound, the devil has taken you captive at his will and snared you.

"In meekness instructing those that oppose themselves; if God peradventure will give them repentance to the acknowledging of the truth; And that they may recover themselves out of the snare of the devil, who are taken captive by him at his will." (II Timothy 2:25–26)

Example of Occult and Witchcraft Curses

Dale was mired in the occult up to his neck; the place where he worked was next to the church. One morning as I was preparing my Sunday message, Dale stuck his head around the half-opened office door and asked me, "Do you know anything about spirits?" I answered, "Yes I do." His desire for help was obvious. I invited him to attend the morning service. He chose not to come. However, a relationship was established between us during the next few months.

It turns out that Dale was heavily involved with a medium in Arizona to whom he had sent much money. As long as the check was in the mail, he had the power to get women of his choice by just setting his eyes on them. His jobs were also attained by this demonic power.

It took Dale several weeks before he came to church, even though his office was next door. He shared with me how difficult it was to get to church. He would drive around the parking lot several times, and finally he would park his car and run into the church. He said, "My it is hard to get here."

Each time we ministered to Dale, he would get more freedom. He invited us out to cleanse his home. We felt a very evil presence as we entered his home and began walking down the hallway. As we approached the washroom, the evil presence got stronger. A sister of faith that operated in the spiritual gift of discerning spirits gave a word of knowledge. This is the altar to Satan that I saw in the spirit before we came. This revelation knowledge caused Dale to admit that it was indeed an altar where he burnt candles to gain power for his evil exploits. The house cleaning and prayer brought Dale more freedom.

Dale came to church one afternoon; he came early for the 6:00 p.m. service. We saw demons manifest all over him. I was prompted by the Holy Spirit to tell Dale to remove the ring from his finger. He removed the ring and passed the ring to me. As he did, the spirit of the medium yelled out, "Didn't I tell you to stay away from this man? He can cast me out, I told you stay away from this (Explicit) man." We cast out the familiar spirit of the medium—Dale was now free. Removal of the ring broke the contact between the medium and Dale.

It is imperative that the one doing the expelling of demons understand their authority in the Lord Jesus Christ. He or she must always be led by the Holy Spirit. The victim being prayed for may not be lucid enough to take part in a prayer of renouncing. The prayer team may just have to go for it.

Generational Curses and Recurring Problems

"Thou shalt not bow down thyself to them, nor serve them: for I the Lord thy God am a jealous God, visiting the iniquity of the fathers upon the children unto the third and fourth generation of them that hate me." (Exodus 20:5)

"And whiles I was speaking, and praying, and confessing my sin and the sin of my people Israel and presenting my suppli-

cation before the Lord my God for the holy mountain of my God." (Daniel 9:20)

"Let thine ear now be attentive, and thine eyes open, that thou mayest hear the prayer of thy servant, which I pray before thee now, day and night, for the children of Israel thy servants, and confess the sins of the children of Israel, which we have sinned against thee: both I and my father's house have sinned." (Nehemiah 1:6)

The inequities of the foreparents must be confessed. Your participation in the iniquities must be confessed and repented of. Note: The repentance is for those that are alive, not for the dead. The soul that sinneth it shall die. You must forgive all foreparents for the iniquities passed down to you. Do not let a root of bitterness develop.

Jesus took upon himself the curse so that all curses may be broken.

"Christ hath redeemed us from the curse of the law, being made a curse for us: for it is written, Cursed is everyone that hangeth on a tree." (Galatians 3:13)

Example of Generational Curses (Testimony)

Jane was the third child of four siblings. Jane's mother had been traumatized as a young adult. The wounds from their mother's trauma prevented proper bonding with the girls born to her. A spirit of rejection was passed down to the children, not allowing proper bonding. This is called Generational Curses or Iniquity.

Rejection at any age allows the strongman of rejection to enter. The strongman of rejection invites other unclean spirits to enter into the soul of the wounded person. Fear of rejection, accusing spirit, self-rejection, a spirit of self-sabotage, a spirit of fear of men, also a spirit of timidity called "shyness."

In Jane's particular case, the spirit of rejection manifested itself through fear of being rejected, a spirit of timidity, and fear of men. Jane states that many times when she is in social settings, the fear of rejection manifest itself through shyness resulting in non-participation in conversations and interaction of others. As a result, this prevents Jane from being truly known by others, being misunderstood, and creating the feelings of being left out and unwanted. A spirit of rejection also creates situations where so-called friends and acquaintances are able to use you for their personal gain.

The fear of men hinders both personal and business relationships. All her life she was uncomfortable around men. The majority of time Jane would keep her distance from men even though she desired a relationship. This creates a feeling of being unlovable. It is very frustrating to fear what you desire. It's even more infuriating to have symptoms of trauma but not know where it came from and how to pinpoint it. If you can't pinpoint the root cause it cannot be fixed. Not being able to connect with men platonic or romantically has been an obstacle to Jane's faith all her life. Ultimately, if God cannot heal this soul wound, then how powerful is He really. Getting rid of the fear of rejection took away the fear of men and rejection allowing Jane to really live out her best life.

Section ll
Provides the steps for action to resolve recurring problems.

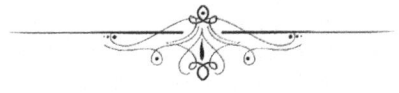

Overcoming Recurring Problems

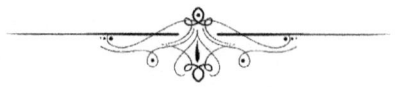

Section II
Solutions Through Deliverance

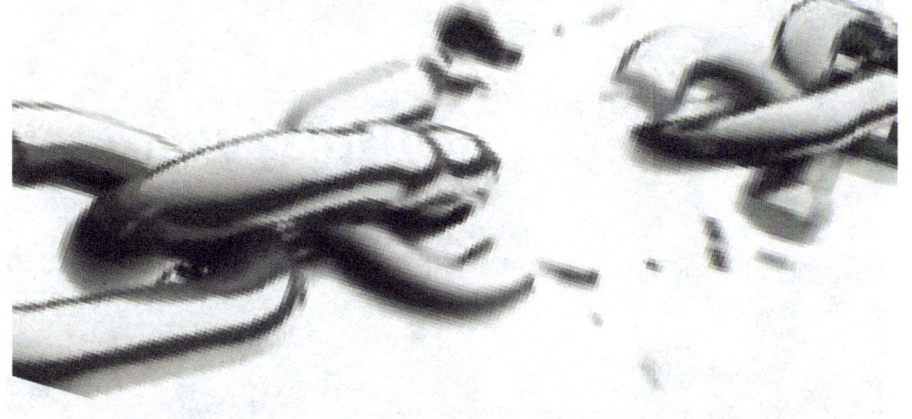

"Warfare Begins When the Confrontation Takes Place

CHAPTER 7

SPIRITUAL WARFARE

- Spiritual warfare, what is it?

"For we wrestle not against flesh and blood, but against principalities, against powers, against the rulers of the darkness of this world, against spiritual wickedness in high places." (Ephesians 6:12)

"Who hath delivered us from the power of darkness, and hath translated us into the kingdom of his dear Son."(Colossians 1:13)

There are two kingdoms, God's kingdom known as the kingdom of light and Satan's kingdom known as the kingdom of darkness. Satan is also known as the god of this world. He as Lucifer was kicked out of heaven because of his rebellion against God. He brought with him one third of the angels that became his servants. Satan and his demons are warrng to keep the ones he has and to gain as many as he can from the kingdom of light.

The action taken by the believer to set the captive free from Satan's kingdom and deliver them to the kingdom of God is warfare.

There is a difference between prayer to God and spiritual warfare prayer. Prayer is the petition we make to God pertaining to our request. Sometimes we include thanksgiving and worshiping in our prayer to God. The believer may pray, fast, memorize scripture, and put on the armor, etc. The believer is to be commended for such Godly activities. Such activity is preparation for warfare. Warfare is what you do to engage and defeat the enemy.

"For we wrestle not against flesh and blood, but against principalities, against powers, against the rulers of the darkness of this world, against spiritual wickedness in high places." (Ephesians 6:12)

"Who hath delivered us from the power of darkness, and hath translated us into the kingdom of his dear son."(Colossians 1:13)

"And when he (Jesus) had called unto him his twelve disciples, he gave them power against unclean spirits, to cast them out, and to heal all manner of sickness and all manner of disease." (Matthew 10:1)

You can see an example of engagement in the author's testimony. "I am a Vietnam Veteran; I was drafted in January of 1969. I completed Basic Training and AIT (Advanced Infantry Training) at Fort Lewis, Washington. By June of 1969, I was in Vietnam. In March of 1970, the Company I was assigned to walked into an ambush. We were engaged in a major fire fight that left some dead and many wounded. I was one of the wounded. I had been in Vietnam since June 1969 and had not engaged the enemy at all. All of the training had prepared me for the engagement; however, I had not engaged the enemy until that day."

The training we are receiving for deliverance is much like Basic Training. We learn about deliverance and overcoming recurring problems. We train then practice with the teacher and Holy Spirit. Finally, we are prepared to engage the enemy.

I thank God for the training and how he prepared me for the engagement of the enemy. Saints, do not allow fear to keep you from engaging the enemy. The unbeliever should not fear coming to Jesus for help with his recurring problems. Jesus' compassion is so great that he wants everybody to experience freedom from recurring problems.

The believer must act on his faith, and the person of doubt can ask God to help him to believe. By coming to Jesus, he will experience mercy, grace, and compassion. The following scriptures shows the compassion of Jesus on all that had a need.

"Jesus said unto him, If thou canst believe, all things are possible to him that believeth. And straightway the father of the child cried out, and said with tears, Lord, I believe; help thou mine unbelief." (Mark 9:23–24 Please read the entire chapter.)

If you find these biblical truths difficult to believe, then come to Jesus, and He will help you overcome your unbelief. He will perform a miracle just for you. The supernatural signs that Jesus performed are for unbelievers as well as believers.

Experience the compassion of Jesus whether you are a believer, unbeliever, skeptic, or an atheist.

"Then Jesus called his disciples unto him, and said, I have compassion on the multitude, because they continue with me now three days, and have nothing to eat: and I will not send them away fasting, lest they faint on the way." (Matthew 15:32)

"And Jesus, moved with compassion, put forth his hand, and touched him, and saith unto him, I will; be thou clean. And as soon as he had spoken, immediately the leprosy departed from him, and he was cleansed." (Mark 1:41–42)

Overcoming Recurring Problems

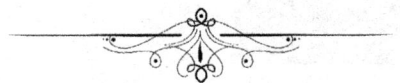

Overcoming Recurring Problems

" *The Weapons of Our Warfare Are Not Carnal*

Chapter 8

EQUIPPED WITH SPIRITUAL WEAPONS

God has equipped his servants with spiritual weapons. These weapons are to be used to tear down demonic strongholds that contribute to recurring problems.

Some weapons are:

- Revelation, knowledge of Jesus (Ephesians 1:17)
- Authority to bind and loose, called keys to the kingdom of heaven (Matthew 16:15–19)
- Power over the devil (Luke 10:19)
- Delivered from the power of darkness (Colossians 1:13)
- Power against unclean spirits (Matthews 10:1)
- Power of the Holy Ghost (Acts 1:8, Acts 2:38)
- A power in us that is greater than the power in the evil one (l John 4:4)
- The nine spiritual gifts of the Holy Ghost (l Corinthians 12:7–10)

The keys to the kingdom of heaven were given to Peter. They were the principles of binding and loosing.

"And I will give unto thee the keys of the kingdom of heaven: and whatever thou shalt bind on earth shall be bound in heaven: and whatever thou shalt loose on earth shall be loosed in heaven." (Matthew 16:19)

Proper knowledge of who Jesus is, is a requirement for operating in the authority needed to bind and loose unclean spirits. The principles of binding and loosing are recorded in Luke.

"When a strongman armed keepeth his palace, his goods are in peace: But when a stronger than he shall come upon him, and overcome him, he taketh from him all his armour wherein he trusted, and divideth his spoils." (Luke 11:21–22)

The servant of the Lord has been given power over the enemy and nothing can hurt him.

"Behold, I give unto you power to tread on serpents and scorpions, and over all the power of the enemy: and nothing shall by any means hurt you." (Luke 10:19)

"And when he had called unto him his twelve disciples, he gave them power against unclean spirits, to cast them out, and to heal all manner of sickness and all manner of disease." (Matthew 10:1)

The believer is fully equiped to use these tools by faith to set the captive free. Faith in the power and using the power is what is needed.

"The Strongman's Palace

CHAPTER 9

THE STRONGMAN AND HIS HOUSE

The strongman is a high-ranking demon spirit that has lower ranking demons under his control. The lower ranking spirits obey the commands of the strongman. These lower ranking spirits make up the armor of the strongman, protecting him, and need to be expelled. The one that is stronger is the person of faith who operates in the power of the Holy Spirit to bind and loose. Any kind of addiction, infirmity, and multiple syndromes can have a strongman directing the recurring problems.

"But if I cast out devils by the spirit of God, then the kingdom of God is come unto you. Or else how can one enter into a strong man's house and spoil his goods, except he first bind the strong man? and then he will spoil his house." (Matthew 12:28–29)

"When a strongman armed keepeth his palace, his goods are in peace: But when a stronger than he shall come upon him, and overcome him, he taketh from him all his armour wherein he trusted, and divideth his spoils." (Luke 11:21–22)

There is much to be learned from the above passage of scriptures about the strongman. He is armed and the keeper of his palace (a large stately house). The goods in the house are kept in place. His armor in which he trusts can be destroyed, and the goods in his house can be spoiled by one stronger than him. The one that is stronger is the Lord Jesus Christ and his anointed believers.

If the person has a strongman spirit of lust, the lust spirit enters first and assumes the position of gatekeeper. The gatekeeper allows other unclean spirits to come in and help him with his evil lust chores. The palace can be occupied with multiple unclean sprits that take orders from the strongman. For example: A spirit requiring multiple sex partners, a spirit of homosexuality, unfaithful to wife spirit, and insatiable sex drive.

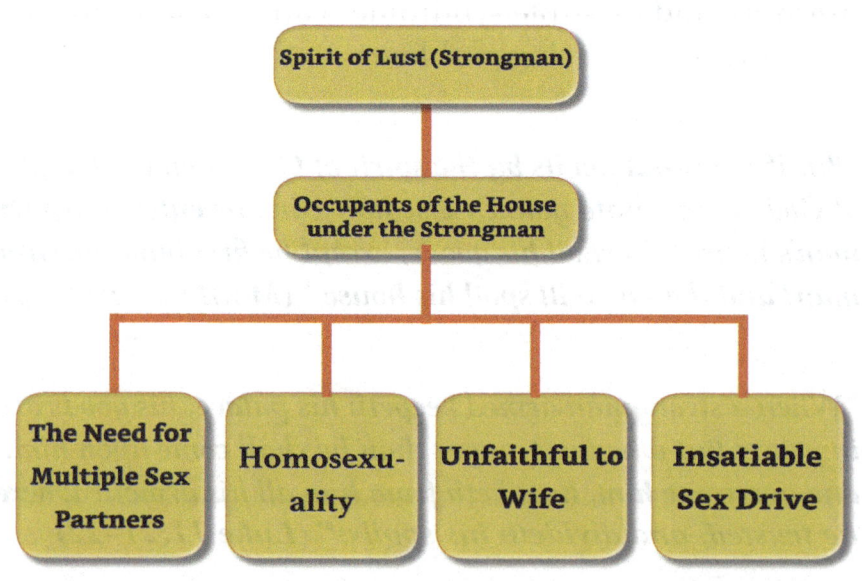

Chapter 10 will demonstrate the binding of the strongman spirit of lust.

Examples of Loosing

A woman loosed from a spirit of infirmity:

> *"And behold, there was a woman which had a spirit of infirmity eighteen years, and was bowed together, and could in no wise lift up herself. And when Jesus saw her, he called her to him, and said unto her, Woman, thou art loosed from thine infirmity. And he laid his hands on her: and immediately she was made straight, and glorified God. And the ruler of the synagogue answered with indignation, because that Jesus had healed on the sabbath day, and said unto the people, There are six days in which men ought to work: in them therefore come and be healed, and not on the sabbath day. The Lord then answered him, and said, Thou hypocrite, doth not each one of you on the sabbath loose his ox or his ass from the stall, and lead him away to watering? And ought not this woman, being a daughter of Abraham, whom Satan hath bound, lo, these eighteen years, be loosed from this bond on the sabbath day? And when he had said these things, all his adversaries were ashamed: and all the people rejoiced for all the glorious things that were done by him." (Luke 13:11–17)*

- The woman in the above scripture had been bound by a spirit of infirmity, which caused a severe curvature of the spine, hunchback.

- She was weak and feeble, unable to lift herself up.

- Jesus said to the woman, "Woman thou art loosed from thine infirmity." And he laid his hands on her, and immediately she was made straight, and glorified God.

- This woman who was the daughter of Abraham was loosed from the infirmity on the Sabbath day. Jesus told the rulers of the synagogue that in like manner as they would loose their ox or ass from the stall for watering, he had loosed the woman from her bondage. Satan had bound her with a spirit of infirmity for 18 years.

Even though the ruler of the synagogue showed indignation because the healing was done on the Sabbath day, he never denied that the woman was healed. Let us take a close look at verse sixteen. The woman was the daughter of Abraham, whom Satan had bound these eighteen years, be loosed from this bond on the Sabbath day.

She had a spirit of infirmity that Satan used to bind her for eighteen years. Satan caused this spirit of infirmity. Jesus loosed her from a sickness that was caused by Satan.

Resurrection of Lazarus

"And when he thus had spoken, he cried with a loud voice, Lazarus, come forth. And he that was dead came forth, bound hand and foot with graveclothes: and his face was bound about

with a napkin. Jesus said unto them, Loose him, and let him go." (John 11:43–44)

Jesus cried with a loud voice *"Lazarus come forth!"* Lazarus came forward still bound with graveclothes. He was resurrected yet bound. Many today have been born again, yet they are still bound with graveclothes.

- Jesus said to them, *"**Loose him, and let him go.**"* Jesus did the impossible, and we do the possible. It was the responsibility of the believers to loose Lazarus of the graveclothes, just as it was necessary for them to roll the stone away.

- Every time we use our authority to loose the person from the graveclothes, we are setting the captive free.

Identify Who the Strongman Is

Ways of identifying the strongman:

1. Spiritual discernment
2. Natural discernment
3. You can ask the spirit to give its name.
4. By tongues and interpretations

1. Spiritual Discernment

The gift of discerning of spirits enables you to supernaturally see into the spirit realm. The gift allows you to accurately see and recognize the unclean spirits. The gift of discerning of spirits works closely with the word of knowledge by the spirit and the word of wisdom by the spirit. The gift of knowledge tells you about the unclean spirit including the name; the gift of wisdom tells you how to use the knowledge.

2. Natural Discernment

There is a level of maturity in which we can tell the difference between good and evil. This maturity comes by exercising of our senses;

"But strong meat belongeth to them that are of full age, even those who by reason of use have their senses exercised to discern both good and evil." (Hebrews 5:14).

A way of using the senses to discern who the strongman is, is by becoming a fruit inspector. A tree is known by the fruit it produces.

"Ye shall know them by their fruits, Do men gather grapes of thorns, or figs of thistles?... Wherefore by their fruits ye shall know them." (Matthew 7:16, 20)

Inspecting the fruit involves the natural use of the senses. What is not revealed through the use of the sense can be discerned by The Holy Spirit and spiritual gifts.

A way of using the senses is by observing the person's behavior and symptoms.

The account of the demonic boy is recorded in this passage of scripture: Mark 9:14–27. The father wanted his son healed. The name used by the father was "he hath a dumb spirit." The father talked about the behavior and symptoms. He asked Jesus to have compassion on us and help us. In Matthew 9:25, Jesus cast out a deaf and dumb spirit. Jesus rebuked the foul spirit, saying unto him, "Thou dumb and deaf spirit, I charge thee. Come out of him and enter no more into him." The father discerned that his son had a dumb spirit. Jesus discerned that the boy had both a deaf and dumb spirit. Jesus discernment was spiritual, and the father's discernment was natural.

3. We can know who the strongman is by asking him to give his name.

"For he (Jesus) said unto him, Come out of the man, thou unclean spirit. And he asked him, What is thy name? And he answered, saying, My name is Legion: for we are many. And he besought him much that he would not send them away out of the country." (Mark 5:8-10)

"And all the devils besought him, saying, Send us into the swine, that we may enter into them." (Mark 5:12)

Jesus knew that the man had an unclean spirit, yet he asked what is your name? Some take an adamant stance against talking to demons under any circumstances. Jesus had quite an intense conversation with Legion. One must not be afraid to walk in Jesus' footsteps in this area of ministry.

4. A seldom used method of getting names of demons and strongmen is speaking in tongues and receiving interpretations from the Holy Spirit. Many demons' names have been given through this spiritual gift of tongues and interpretation. This is a valuable tool in the deliverance ministry.

Strongmen Listed in the Bible

- Spirit of Divination
- Spirit of Fear
- Spirit of Heaviness
- Spirit of Whoredom
- Spirit of Bondage
- Spirit of Infirmity
- Unclean Spirit
- Dumb and Deaf
- Familiar Spirit
- Spirit of Jealousy
- Spirit of Error
- Spirit of Death
- Lying Spirit
- Perverse Spirit
- Spirit of Haughtiness

This is only a partial list.

Overcoming Recurring Problems

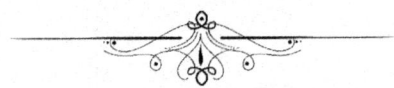

Overcoming Recurring Problems

"
Set the Captive Free

Chapter 10

Steps to Deliverance; Expelling of Strongman (Demons)

1. Identify the problem.
Please do not overlook the doctor's diagnosis. The medical diagnosis can be used to help determine the natural or biological causes. They can also help you know how to pray.

Determine spiritual cause by the methods listed in the previous chapter.

2. Fall out of agreement with the strongman.
"Can two walk together, except they be agreed." (Amos 3:3)

3. Renounce the strongman and any demon associated with it.

I refuse to follow, obey, or recognize you anymore.

The need to renounce became clear to me while I was praying for a victim to be free from a demon. I commanded the demon "to come out." I repeated the command several times, and it did not leave. I said to the demon, "I command you to go. What gives you the right to stay?" The demon said, "I don't have to go, he is enjoying the pleasure derived from my being here, he likes me being here." We were successful in casting the demon out once the victim renounced it.

4. Repent of my participation in the activity (sin) that allowed the unclean spirit to come in.

Sin deprives us of any protection from God.

"If we confess our sins, he is faithful and just to forgive us our sins, and to cleanse us from all unrighteousness."
 (1 John 1:9)

5. Bind the strongman and loose (means cast out) him from the victim.

Be sure to spoil the house of all lesser demons occupying it. They too must be cast out. Never allow a bound spirit to remain in the person. Be sure to cast them out too. Believe that the blood of Jesus cleanses you. Bind the strongman and spoil his house.

How to bind the strongman ... Say to the strongman, "By the authority given me from the Lord Jesus Christ, I bind the strongman of lust. I tie you up with spiritual bonds, I bind your power to perform your assignment in the person anymore. By the authority I have in the name of the Lord Jesus Christ, I command the spirit of lust to come out now."

6. Pray for healing. Now that you have bound and

loosed the unclean spirits of infirmity from the person, you should pray for healing.

Expelling can result in miraculous healing, but when it doesn't happen immediately, do not be disappointed. Healing is on its way when all foreign entities have been expelled.

Early in my career, I worked refinishing pianos and furniture. I would use steel wool and mineral spirits to clean the stripped surfaces. One day while cleaning a piano, I got a piece of steel wool in my hand. Although it was a very small piece, it caused much pain for over a year. One day, I squeezed the pus around the site of the wound and out came a little piece of steel wool. After the steel wool was removed, healing took place. Healing only takes place after the foreign entities have been removed.

7. Declare faith in the one that has set you free.

"But if I cast out devils by the Spirit of God, then the kingdom of God is come unto you." (Matthew 12:28)

"And when he was come into the ship, he that had been possessed with the devil prayed him that he might be with him." Howbeit Jesus suffered him not, but saith unto him, Go home to thy friends, and tell them how great things the Lord hath done for thee, and hath had compassion on thee."

(Mark 5:18-19)

He wanted to spend time with Jesus. He was told to go home to his friends and tell them how great things the Lord has done for him and Jesus had compassion on him.

We call this testifying about what God has done for you.

I encourage people who have been delivered to testify about what has been done. When asked what happened to you, many say, "Oh I just got prayed for." No, you were not just prayed for, demons were cast out, and now you are walking in the new freedom it has brought you.

"Whosoever therefore shall confess me before men, him will I confess also before my Father which is in heaven. But whosoever shall deny me before men, him will I also deny before my Father which is in heaven." (Matthew 10:32-33)

Those of you that have been touched by the hand of God, don't be fearful of sharing all that has been done for you.

How to Bind a Demon or Strongman

- How to Bind the Strongman:

Make a declaration:

Say to the strongman, "By the authority I have in the name of the Lord Jesus Christ, I bind you. I tie you up with spiritual bonds. I bind your power to perform your assignment in this person. Strongman of lust you are bound. I bind the lesser demons occupying the house under the authority of the strongman."

Overcoming Recurring Problems

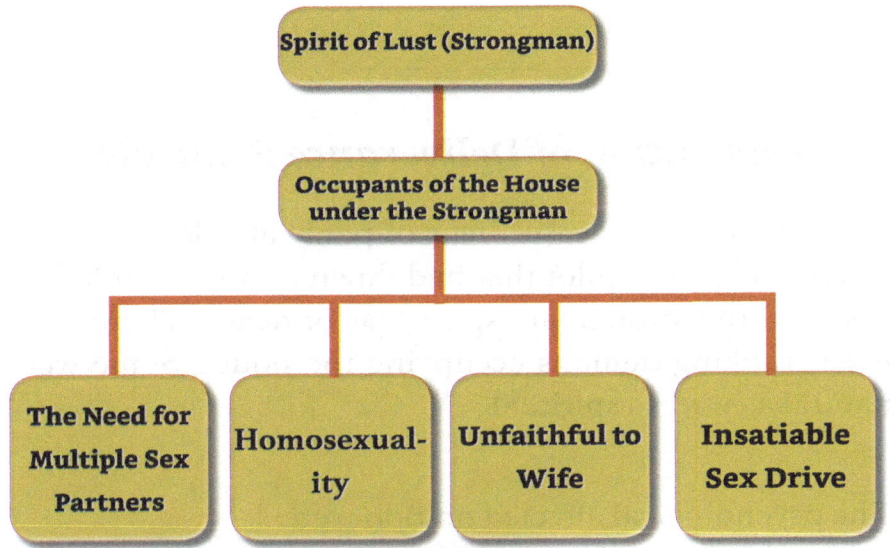

Prayer Leader:

I bind the need for multiple sex partners.

I bind the homosexual spirit.

I bind the unfaithfulness to wife spirit.

I bind the insatiable sex drive spirit and spoil the house. I expel all the demons occupying the house under the strongman of lust. Once you have expelled the spirit that made up the armor, then kick out (loose) the strongman of lust.

Binding the demons of lower rank in the house is spoiling the strongman's armor. The strongman is weakened as the house is spoiled, making it possible for the strongman to be cast out (loose). This is an example of how binding is done. This has worked for us. However, we want the person praying (prayer leader) to be led by the Holy Spirit.

Application of Deliverance Principles

Let us revisit Bob's case—fear of panic attack in Chapter Three. Bob was a pilot that had flown hundreds of hours. Bob had the strongman, spirit fear of death. There were lesser ranking demons occupying the house; Some were natural as well as spiritual.

The psychological affected on Bob were:
1. Phobia
2. Sense of impending doom
3. Sense of danger
4. Fear of loss of control
5. Fear of death

Bob's physiological symptoms were:
1. Sweaty palms
2. Trembling
3. Shaking
4. Shortness of breath
5. Chest pain
6. Dizziness
7. Rapid heartbeat

Fear of having a panic attack was so intense that Bob

grounded himself from flying. The plane sat unused in the hangar It was determined that the root cause of Bob's panic attack was the fear of death. The strongman was a spirit fear of death in Bob.

To prepare Bob for deliverance prayer, we told him he must do the following things. Bob must be the one speaking these words.

Bob began to participate by saying out loud:

- I, Bob, fall out of agreement with the strongman fear of death.
- I, Bob, renounce the spirit fear of death.
- I, Bob, repent of my participation with fear of death.
- I, Bob, believe the blood of Jesus cleanses me.

The authority of the believer sets him free, and the blood of Jesus cleanses him. This ends Bob's initial participation. He submits to the prayer leader.

Prayer Leader:

- In the name of Jesus and by the authority I have, I bind the strongman of fear of death. I tie you up and spoil your house.

- I bind the lower ranking demon by the authority I have in the name of Jesus Christ.

- Fear of flying, I command you to loose Bob now by the authority I have in the name of Jesus Christ.

- Fear of harm to my son and I command you, loose now, come out by the authority I have in the name of Jesus Christ.

- Fear of clouds, I command you to come out by the authority I have in the name of Jesus Christ.

- Fear of panic attacks, I command you to come out by the authority I have in the name of Jesus Christ.

- I now use my authority to cast out the strongman, the spirit of fear of death. Come out now, loose now, be gone now.

Overcoming Recurring Problems

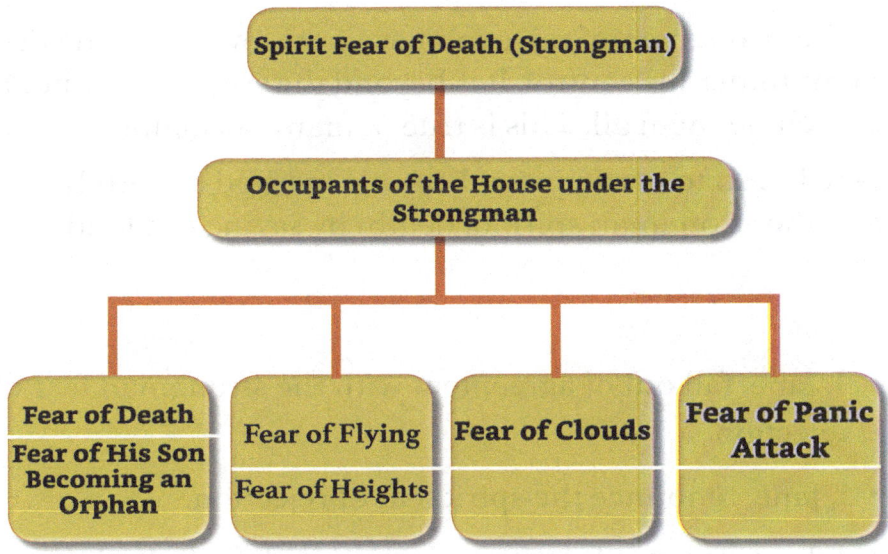

If there is no other spirit revealed, then you pray for healing. If there are other strongmen present, then repeat the procedure starting with Bob falling out of agreement, etc. This procedure can be used against all addictive spirits, paranoia, addictive behavior, murdering spirit, destructive spirit, mental illness spirit, infirmity spirit, etc. Pray that the Holy Spirit will reveal any other unclean spirit. These contribute to the recurring problems.

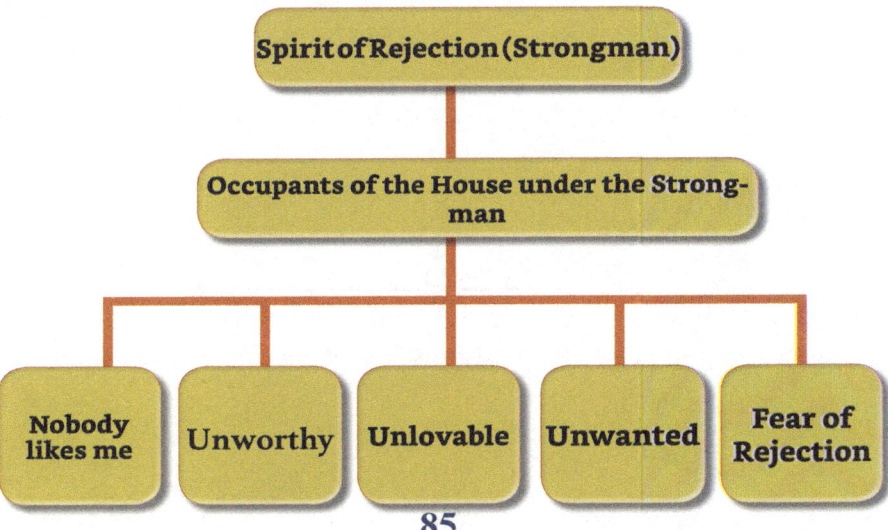

The strongman of rejection has many lower ranking demons under his control. It is beyond the scope of this book to include them all. This is true of many strongmen.

Jane began to participate (the same method as with Bob and the strongman spirit of death) by saying out loud:

- I, Jane, fall out of agreement with the strongman fear of rejection.
- I, Jane, renounce the spirit fear of rejection.
- I, Jane, repent of my participation with fear of rejection.
- I, Jane, believe the blood of Jesus cleanses me.

The authority of the believer sets her free, and the blood of Jesus cleanses her. This ends Jane's initial participation. Jane submits to the prayer leader.

Prayer Leader:

- *In the name of Jesus and by the authority I have, I bind nobody likes me, I command you to lose Jane now.*

- *Fear of unworthiness, I command you, loose now, come out by the authority I have in the name of Jesus Christ.*

- *Fear of being unlovable, I command you to come out by the authority I have in the name of Jesus Christ.*

- *Fear of being unwanted, I command you to come out by the authority I have in the name of Jesus, loose now.*

- *Fear of rejection, I command you to come out by the authority I have in the name of Jesus Christ.*

- *I now use my authority to cast out the strongman, the spirit of fear of rejection. Come out now, loose now, be gone now.*

If there are no other spirits revealed, then you pray for healing. If there are other strongmen present, then repeat the procedure starting with Jane's falling out of agreement, etc. This procedure can be used against all addictive spirits, paranoia, addictive behavior, murdering spirit, destructive spirit, mental illness spirit, infirmity spirit, etc. Pray that the Holy Spirit will reveal any other unclean spirit. These contribute to the recurring problems.

Follow the example with Bob and Jane to cast out spirit of fear and the lesser ranking demons.

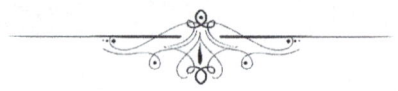

Overcoming Recurring Problems

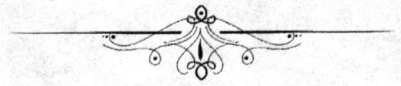

Overcoming Recurring Problems

" *New Identity, New Mind*

Chapter 11

Recommended Actions After Deliverance

Pray for Healing of All Wounds

1. Pray for Healing.

Healing only takes place after the steel wool has been removed or expelled. It does not matter what the nature of the entity is. Jesus died for your healing,

"Who his own self bare our sins in his own body on the tree, that we, being dead to sins, should live unto righteousness; for by whose stripes ye were healed." (I Peter 2:24)

2. Testify.

"But if I cast out Devils by the spirit of God, then the Kingdom of God is come unto you." (Matthew 12:28)

"And when he was come into the ship, he that had been possessed with the devil prayed him and he might be with him. Howbeit

Jesus suffered him not, but sayeth unto him, Go home to thy friends, and tell them how great things the Lord has done for thee, and hath had compassion on thee." (Mark 5:8–19)

In the above scripture, he that had been possessed wanted to spend time with Jesus. He was told to go home to his friends and report to his friends what great things the Lord had done for him. We called this testifying what God has done in your life. We encourage you to testify about all that has been done.

Those of you who have been touched by the hand of God, don't be fearful of sharing all that has been done for you.

"Whosoever therefore shall confess me before men, him will I confess also before my Father which is in heaven. But whosoever shall deny me before men, him will I also deny before my Father which is in heaven." (Matthew 10:32–33)

3. Declare your faith in the one that has set you free and become born again.

"Nicodemus saith unto to him, how can a man be born when he is old? Can he enter the second time into his mother's womb, and be born? Jesus answered, Verily, verily, I say unto thee, Except a man be born of water and of the Spirit, he cannot enter into the Kingdom of God. That which is born of flesh is flesh; and that which is born of the Spirit is spirit. Marvel not that I said unto thee, Ye must be born again. The wind bloweth where it listeth, and thou hearest the sound thereof, but canst

not tell whence it cometh, and whither it goeth: So is everyone that is born of the Spirit." (John 3:4–8)

"That if thou shall confess with thy mouth the Lord Jesus, and shalt believe in thine heart that God hath raised him from the dead, thou shalt be saved. For with the heart man believeth unto righteousness; and with the mouth confession is made unto salvation." (Romans 10:9–10)

"Then Peter said unto them, Repent, and be baptized every one of you in the name of Jesus Christ for the remission of sins, and ye shall receive the gift of the Holy Ghost. For the promise is unto you, and to your children, and to all that are afar off, even as many as the Lord our God shall call. And with many other words did he testify and exhort, saying, Save yourselves from this untoward generation. Then they that gladly received his word were baptized: and the same day there were added unto them about three thousand souls." (Acts 2:38–41)

4. Do not return to the way of darkness once you have been delivered.

"As a dog return it to his vomit, so a fool returning to his folly." (Proverbs 26:11)

"But it is happened unto them according to the true proverb, The dog is turned to his own vomit again; And the sow that was washed to her wallowing in the mire." (ll Peter 2:22)

5. Attend a Bible believing church that teaches and preach-

es the word in its fullness, including deliverance and expelling demons.

6. Commit to reading the word of God daily.

7. Develop your relationship with the Lord Jesus Christ.

8. Renew the mind.

"I beseech you therefore, brethren, by the mercies of God, that ye present your bodies a living sacrifice, holy, acceptable unto God, which is your reasonable service. And be not conformed to this world: but be ye transformed by the renewing of your mind, that ye may prove what is that good, and acceptable, and perfect, will of God." (Romans 12:1–2)

Renewing the Mind

Renewing the mind is a daily requirement as you walk out your new life in Christ. Renewing the mind is replacing all lies of the devil with the truth of God's word. It is bringing every thought into captivity and obedience to Christ.

"Casting down imaginations, and every high thing that exalteth itself against the knowledge of God, and bringing into captivity every thought to the obedience of Christ." (ll Corinthians 10:5)

Renewing the mind is replacing the old programming received while in the kingdom of darkness with the truth of the Kingdom of light.

"Therefore if any man be in Christ, he is a new creature: old things are passed away; behold, all things are become new." (ll Corinthians 5:17)

"I beseech you therefore, brethren, by the mercies of God, that ye present your bodies a living sacrifice, holy, acceptable unto God, which is your reasonable service. And be not conformed to this world: but be ye transformed by the renewing of your mind, that ye may prove what is that good, and acceptable, and perfect, will of God." (Romans 12:1-2)

"Who hath delivered us from the power of darkness, and hath translated us into the kingdom of his dear Son." (Colossians 1:13)

"Wherein time past ye walked according to the course of his world, according to the prince of the power of the air, the spirit that now worketh in the children of disobedience." (Ephesians 2:2)

Now that we are born again, it is needful to replace the old way of thinking with the word of God.

Replace the old programming (way of thinking) with the word of God. Learn to think like, speak like, and act like what the word of God says you are. The new way of thinking must be believed and acted on.

"Therefore if any man be in Christ, he is a new creature: old things are passed away; behold, all things are become new."
 (II Corinthians 5:17)

Once we have been delivered, we are not to return to the old ways of darkness (See II Peter 2:22).

You are to put off the old man and be renewed in your mind, then you will be able to think like Christ, speak like Christ, walk like Christ, and do the things that Christ did.

Who you are in Christ is explained in the scriptures below

I Am . . .

1. A child of God. (Romans 8:16)
2. Redeemed from the hand of the enemy. (Psalms 107:2)
3. Forgiven. (Colossians 1:13–14)
4. Saved by grace through faith. (Ephesians 2:5)
5. Justified. (Romans 5:1)
6. Sanctified. (I Corinthians 6:11)
7. A New Creature. (II Corinthians 5:17)
8. Partaker of His Divine Nature. (II Peter 1:4)

9. Redeemed from the Curse of the Law. (Galatians 3:13)

10. Delivered from the powers of darkness. (Colossians 1:13)

11. Led by the Spirit of God. (Romans 8:14)

12. A Son of God. (Romans 8:14)

13. Kept in safety wherever I go. (Psalms 91:11)

14. Getting all my needs met by Jesus. (Philippians 4:19)

15. Casting all my cares on Jesus. (l Peter 5:7)

16. Strong in the Lord and in the power of His Might. (Ephesians 6:10)

17. Doing all things through Christ who strengthens me. (Philippians 4:13)

18. An heir of God and a joint heir with Jesus. (Romans 8:17)

19. Heir to the blessings of Abraham. (Galatians 3:13–14)

20. Observing and doing the Lord's commandments. (Deuteronomy 28:12)

21. Blessed coming in and going out. (Deuteronomy 28:6)

22. An inheritor of eternal life. (l John 5:11–12)

23. Blessed with all spiritual blessings. (Ephesians 1:3)

24. Healed by His stripes. (l Peter 2:24)

25. Exercising my authority over the enemy. (Luke 10:19)

26. Above only and not beneath. (Deuteronomy 28:13)

27. More than a conqueror. (Romans 8:37)

Overcoming Recurring Problems

28. Establishing God's Word here on earth. (Matthew 16:19)

29. An overcomer by the Blood of the Lamb and Word of my Testimony. (Revelations 12:11)

30. Daily overcoming the devil. (l John 4:4)

31. Not moved by what I see. (ll Corinthians 4:18)

32. Walking by faith and not by sight. (ll Corinthians 5:7)

33. Casting down vain imaginations. (ll Corinthians 10:4–5)

34. Bringing every thought into captivity. (ll Corinthians 10:5)

35. Being transformed by a renewed mind. (Romans 12:1–2)

36. A laborer together with God. (l Corinthians 3:9)

37. The righteousness of God in Christ.
38. (ll Corinthians 5:21)

39. An imitator of Jesus. (Ephesians 5:1)

40. Light of the World. (Matthews 5:14)

Knowing who we are in Christ is reflected in the above scriptures. It takes obedience to maintain our freedom along with action. Without action we are incomplete in our discipleship with our Lord Jesus Christ.

Testimonies and Endorsements

Hi Brother Mel:

Over the past several years, I've sent you about a dozen people who were bound to demonic strongholds. Thank you so much for your time with them! As you know, many of them saw a demonic manifestation as you prayed. Congratulations on your book, Healing by Deliverance. In the past, I've been to weekend conferences on deliverance with Peter and Doris Wagner and read "how-to-do-it books" on casting out demons and deliverance ministry. Some of them were by Neil Anderson, Frank Hammond, Derek Prince, Don Dickerman, and Marilyn Hickey. As an author myself, published by HarperCollins/Thomas Nelson Publishing, I want to compliment you! In my opinion, yours is the clearest, simplest explanation on deliverance of all these heroes of the faith! I will be recommending it to people I disciple in Greece, India, the U.S. etc.

In His Service,

Terry Felber

Author of Am I Making Myself Clear and The Legend of the Monk and the Merchant

Overcoming Recurring Problems

Dear Brother Mel,

Recently, after almost 50 years of operating in a God-given Gift of Healing and seeing many miracles, I visited with my friend of many years, Brother Mel.

He startled me by his commands of "Kirk, you need some deliverance." No one had ever told me that all those years. On the contrary, I had been involved in many deliverances for others. Knowing him well enough not to doubt him, I agreed.

In my first session with him, a spirit of "rejection" left me. When I arrived home afterward, I was even more surprised to see my wife looking like a new person to me. Having rid my life of the spirit of rejection, some kind of spiritual haze came off of me, and I could see her in new and wonderful ways that I had never seen in 55 years of marriage. It has taken a year to address all the hurts inflicted on my wife through this spirit operating through me. I had been so blinded to the hurts I had inflicted on her and others thinking how loving I was to everyone. Lately, the relationship has been experiencing a great deal of healing and is considerably beyond what it had been. We are experiencing restoration of the years the Locust have eaten.

It is an understatement to say that Satan is a deceiver. I believe Brother Mel's gift of deliverance is a needed gift to our community for those seeking their own freedom.

Today, I have prayer time that I have sought for years. God is calling me to Him in wonderful ways, and I am now free to respond more fully than ever.

To say all of this, takes a man of God, gifted accordingly, to the one teaching about this ministry. May everyone reading the short story be deeply blessed.

Kirk Winkelmeyer

I am beyond grateful for Brother Mel, his deliverance ministry, and his book, Healing by Deliverance. At the recommendation of a Christian medical doctor, I visited Brother Mel for deliverance. My life is forever changed because I received astonishing deliverance and healing. Additionally, Brother Mel's biblical teaching equipped me to go forth and spread the truth about deliverance and healing and equipped me to successfully pray for deliverance and healing for myself and others. Previously, I had read several other books on spiritual warfare and deliverance, but their methods were complicated, and sometimes the biblical accuracy was questionable. Brother Mel explains the biblical truth of deliverance in a simple, clear manner. The countless testimonies of deliverance and healing in the name of our Lord Jesus Christ confirm these teachings. Thank you, Brother Mel, for listening carefully to the Holy Spirit and bringing clarity to this often-misinterpreted subject. Thank you, Lord, for helping us to understand, experience, and apply the truth.

Angie S.

Dear Brother Mel,

Your current book, Healing by Deliverance, is a great benefit to people like me who were experiencing recurring problems that could not be addressed by any other types of intervention, including medical interventions like surgery, searching the scriptures, and even years of prayer. Your writings are founded on scriptures that you share with the reader. The way you present it is also very practical and enables a person to put into practice these biblical truths. This helps people experience the freedom in Christ that the scriptures promised. Personally, I now use the concepts that you teach on an almost daily basis. I have seen myself, my family, and others set free to pursue God's calling in their lives.

So, I look forward to the impact that your new book will have on the advancement of God's Kingdom.

Be blessed and encouraged!

Brian Mullan

NOW IT'S YOUR TURN

Discover the EXACT three-step blueprint you need to become a bestselling author in as little as three months.

Self-Publishing School helped me, and now I want them to help you with this FREE resource to begin outlining your book!

Even if you're busy, bad at writing, or don't know where to start, you CAN write a bestseller and build your best life.

With tools and experience across a variety of niches and professions,

Self-Publishing School is the only resource you need to

take your book to the finish line!

DON'T WAIT

Say "YES" to becoming a bestseller:

https://self-publishingschool.com/friend/

Overcoming Recurring Problems

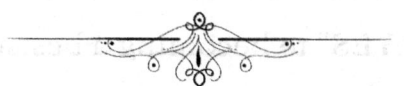

About the Author

Melvin was born in Arkansas and reared on a farm in the Mississippi Delta. He finished high school at the age of sixteen. He earned a BS degree from the University of Arkansas at Pine Bluff, Arkansas. He was accepted in the Graduate School at Colorado State University the summer of 1967.

His graduate program was interrupted nearly two years while he served his country in Vietnam. In March of 1970, his unit walked into an ambush. He was wounded and received a Purple Heart and a Bronze Star.

He returned to CSU and completed his MS degree in Plant Science. Shortly after completing his master's degree, he started a Bible Study on CSU campus called "Campus Bible Study." During Christmas break of 1973, he had his first encounter with the demonic. Seven unclean spirits were cast out of a young lady.

God told him to study the scriptures of Jesus' ministry of setting the captive free. Forty-eight years later, he is still obedient to God's calling. He is founder and Pastor of All Nations Church and Deliverance Center, Fort Collins Colorado. Hundreds of souls have been set free through his deliverance ministry. Pastor Johnson has ministered in South Africa, Mexico as well as the United States. He is available for seminars, conferences, speaking engagements and deliverance sessions. The first book written by Pastor Melvin Johnson, Healing by Deliverance: A Handbook on How to Cast out Demons, was self-published and can now be purchased on Amazon.

Overcoming Recurring Problems

NOTES

NOTES

Overcoming Recurring Problems

NOTES

Made in the USA
Monee, IL
22 June 2025

19837578R00066